Much of the text is about how to fight wars without actually having to do battle: it gives tips on how to outsmart one's opponent so that physical battle is not necessary. As such, it has found application as a training guide for many competitive endeavors that do not involve actual combat.

There are business books applying its lessons to "office politics" and corporate strategy. Many Japanese companies make the book required reading for their key executives. The book is also popular among Western business management, who have turned to it for inspiration and advice on how to succeed in competitive business situations.

The Art of War has been the subject of various law books and legal articles on the trial process, including negotiation tactics and trial strategy.

Depiction in media

The Art of War, by Stephen Jeffreys, is a dramatic interpretation incorporating recitations from the text with the telling of two stories: one of a US commander in the Iraq War and the other of a group of Australian company executives. The play was commissioned by the Sydney Theatre Company for their resident "Actor's Company" of twelve actors. It was first performed in May 2007.

Brøderbund Software published games based on Sun Tzu's The Art of War. The first, entitled The Ancient Art of War, the second, The Ancient Art of War at Sea. They are simulation games, with strategy, geography and adventure. They were released on computers including Apple II (First title only), Macintosh, and DOS.

The Art of War is a 2000 film starring Wesley Snipes, which uses the text as rough motivation for the plot. It was followed by two straight-to-DVD sequels.

Swedish metal band Sabaton named their fifth album The Art of War after the book, and the album feature quotes from the book as introductions to several tracks.

The History Channel aired a documentary in 2009 that discussed Sun Tzu's principles pertaining to the Vietnam War, Operation Overlord, and the Battle of Gettsyburg, as well as Sun Tzu's leading the Kingdom of Wu army against the Kingdom of Chu.

The Art of War is referenced extensively in the Oliver Stone movie Wall Street.

There is also an upcoming graphic novel adaption of The Art of War, planned to be published by It Books in summer 2010.

In 1996, a 13 episodes TV series based on Sun Tzu's life story, titled Sun Wu, was produced, starring Sun Yanjun as Sun Tzu.

In 2008, producer Zhang Jizhong adapted Sun Tzu's life story into a 40-episodes historical drama TV series titled Bing Sheng; aka The Ultimate Master of War: Sun Tzu), starring Zhu Yawen as Sun Tzu.

Printed in Great Britain
by Amazon

tortured elephants

A SHORT COLLECTION OF POLITICAL POETRY

MANVĪR SINGH

"For truth is ugly."

— Nietzsche

ISBN: 9798854340069

@stayinsyncwithyourinstincts

"no one is free
who has not obtained
the empire of himself..."

— Pythagorus

***

"sang sakhā sabh thaj gcae
koū na nibehyo sāth"

all associates and companions have deserted me;
no one's support remains;

"kāhu Nānak ehē bipath mēy
ttēk ēk raghūnāth"

o' Nanak, in this tragedy,
the Mighty Spirit alone is my support.

— Guru Tēgh Bāhādur

9

The old became lost,
the new proved useless;
we burned the bridge,
and sank the boat.

There is no going back,
only braving the way ———
come what may, come what may.

98

History
is not a neat,
tidy arrangement
of indisputable facts —
history involves getting
down and dirty, into
dark pits of
the past.

१५

one won't renounce the kingdom of Maya
founded in the lower nature of man
merely because one *must*;
one gives up worldliness
because one discovers
there is something
more permanent,
more important,
more desirable.

I once met a crazy woman;
no child, no man, no home;
a gaze which could melt steel;
she was always armed to the bone.

She told me I must be the iron
no magnet could resist;
"you've already strayed from the path,
the moment you think you've finished."

She said: "beware of all the holy books,
and all the creeds and schools,
and every law that man has made,
and all the golden rules."

"People want to hear in songs
the words they're afraid to say;
how your desire for wildness could
the sorrow of a paycheck allay?"

"The world of men, which is a mob;
the mob, which is a shrew —
cares only for the end achieved,
and not the means you use."

Two wolves and a lamb
deciding on *what's for lunch*;
tortured elephants and a caged lion;
legions of pedophilic clowns in neckties;
communal narcissism, absence of glory;
a child's prayer to be delivered from
the evils of suburbia; and inept
irrationalists claiming life to
be an emergent property in
a random arrangement
of dead atoms…
"Democracy"

Man judges everything
in relation to himself:
what's bigger than him is big,
what's smaller than him is small.

One thing's certain:
man's *a part* of the spectacle — not *apart*.

Everyone finds his own role.

Do not bother with
the middle man.
Prophets are pocketed by
the middle man.
The devil sends, in his stead:
the middle man.

२०

I was told I didn't have the nerves,
I told them a cheerful abdomen
ought to pick up the slack;

I am told I will lose everything,
I tell them it is all mine
to give back.

prophecies are a complete fabrication;
no one has ever seen the future!
how can one know the future
if the future doesn't even
know the future?
and yet...
while the future
cannot be predicted,
anybody who makes the claim
that the future cannot be predicted
is, really, making a prediction
about the future.

false prophets and cannibals
in a world of child-kings!
your guru is the raft
that will ferry you
through it all.

Modern day events
can only be understood
if we trace their implications
with a direct line from
the earliest records
of antiquity.

If history be not ancient fable,
ask the Freemasons and they'll tell you,
despite not knowing a thing about stonework
themselves — they have descended from
builders of the Tower of Babel!

To the culturally, religiously, and
racially self-aware rulers of the world,
the history of millennia ago is
treated like breaking news...
and there *you* are, under
the impression that WW2
was a *long time ago.*

the executioner refused to let the prisoner
hang by way of the standard-drop method,
and argued that the prisoner would suffer
a far crueler death and yet would not
be asphyxiated any sooner; the warden
and the gathered crowd, both peasants
and nobles alike, were all displeased, but
without any of the necessary preparations
for a long-drop, it was at last decided
that the very best way to deal with
the situation was to simply
behead the guilty party.

the executioner complied
and sharpened his axe while
everyone waited, including the prisoner.

when the time came, the prisoner
was made a disingenuous offer
to say his last words in brief:

> "I really did not think they would put
> a young gentleman to *death*
> for such a trifle! ——"

the crowd was hysterical to see the
executioner manage his job in one strike.

२४

Oh,
and…
how did
heterosexuals
end up in the closet?

after training, and before cage time, ada's
parents would teach her how to play
strategic "war games" using the
maps of foreign countries.

by the age of seven, she'd been made to kill
kittens; despite shaking for days, praise
from her commanders remedied all ills.

by the age of nine, she could put together
a handgun in her sleep, and wringing
the necks of kittens had become
child's play.

by the age of fifteen: forced hand-to-hand
combat before a crowd of spectators,
and punishment for every loss.

by twenty, ada was a murderer
programmed with command codes
and an agonizing compulsion to obey.

ada's parents succeeded in their project
and figured that they'd do it again,
but that *this time*, they would try
going less for 'killing machine'
and more for 'sex slave'.

૨૬

Who is there
that escapes criticism?

I sharpened the sickle before the sword,
and made my day last a hundred years;
I tried to nourish extravagant hope,
but all I did was relay my fears.

Stuck between being and not to be ———
he who serves a revolution plows the sea.

To their *"peaceful"* uses of industry,
there's no solution still;
what revolutions won't do,
evolution will.

So I sharpen the sickle before the sword
and make my day last a hundred years;
I try to nourish extravagant hope,
but all I do is relay my fears.

Stuck between being and not to be ———
he who serves a revolution plows the sea.

only when the super rich,
when the rulers in the shadows,
are declared *excommunicate* for their
crimes against the People,
can we finally be in
some position to
create Eden —
inheritance tax,
and sending all the
merchants and politicians
who vote in favor of war
to sail towards suffering and
help dig the trenches, whilst the common
women seize their Bohemian Groves
armed on horseback! Indeed,
brainstorming is essential…
before we make rebellion
we must think rebellion;
planning is indeed
half the job.

I protected my naiveté
and saved a seat at the table
between Rousseau and Whitman,
where we convinced ourselves
that man is basically noble
and only twisted by
institutions;
then, once
the moment
of payments and
liberation from the past
arrived, how did we finally pay
for everything we had and
everything we were?
with *ceremony*.

hey, rockstar! —
have you got nothing
to say for yourself?
have some grace
and step out of
the limelight.
re-value
your values!
you put security
before truth, and this
is why you are
small.

Every *nation* of peoples,
like every individual, has
a psychological profile;
you dare call a man
mentally ill?
Dare to go
one step
further.

we know Nietzsche criticized much,
but what did he advocate?
Nietzsche advocated the union
of Dionysian and Apollonian forces.

Dionysus would provide
group ecstasy and holy intoxication,
enabling the wildness within *all of us*;
Apollo would provide contemplation,
art, and exercise of reason for
the cultured *individual*.

Balance is born when Apollo
harnesses the mastī of Dionysus.

wah, hey guru!

33

The spirit of War
has been procured
by hoggish credit-lend'rs ———
aye, these be the *Banksters*...

to the Bankster,
war is the richest harvest;

to the Bankster,
war heals all wounds;

to the Bankster,
the faults of the burglar
are qualities worth aspiring for.

Consider the wisdom
of France's Phillip the Fair,
and nab them all at once!

38

No history
is so hard to write
as that of our *own* times;
the task is even more difficult
if one attempts to narrate events
in which they have taken part.
Fortunately for me,
I grew up with
television.
Huh?

The guru appeared
to the disciple in a dream;
the disciple honored the guru,
and swore to do his bidding in this world.
Before being woken from his sleep,
all the disciple heard was:

"You often symbolize slavery by chains, but
chains can be physical, mental, or spiritual.

Surely: a slave is held most securely when
he's held by the chains of his own fears, and
by his own slavish desire for bodily comfort."

The next morning,
following his *nitnēm*, the disciple
began digging a hole to build a root cellar.

you wish to keep a secret? don't tell a friend;
3 can keep a secret, if 2 of them are dead;
yes, let your standards be high instead;
for "follow your heart" is Hell's
most effective slogan yet.

in July of 1856, the then-prime-minister of
Britain stood up in Parliament and said:

"there is a power we seldom mention
in this House —— I mean secret societies.
its's useless to deny, because impossible
to conceal, that a great part of Europe
(to say nothing of other countries)
is covered with a network of these
secret societies just as the superficies of
the earth are covered with railroads.
and what are their objects?
they do not attempt
to conceal their
ambitions…"

another member of Parliament
is reported to have then interrupted,
without bothering to rise, anonymously:

"or… we
could talk *instead*
of how submissively
the Chinese are taking to poppy!"

There can be no mercy for Britain.

because the pirates had always moved
in secrecy, the public never knew of them;
because the public never knew of the pirates,
they were fooled into thinking that
stooge-kings and local sophists
were the real head-men
in charge of all.

because pirate funded
specialization of intellect
made the keen sense of pirates obsolete, gold
piled up elsewhere, and the pirates went
extinct; out of their demise
rose forth the bankster lords
and the first world war.

all in all:
there can be no mercy
for the *Low Countries* either.
There's a time for arriving,
and a time for going;
the time for going
is now arriving.

"The Great Pirates"

Specialization
is in fact just
a fancy form
of slavery
wherein the
'expert'
is fooled
into accepting
his slavery
by way of an
illusory carrot:
being 'secure'
for life.

In truth,
only the king's son
receives the whole
kingdom-wide
scope of training.

Your 'experts' are
the blind men of Buddha
molesting the poor elephant.

80

in virtue
of *what law,*
divine or otherwise,
should those who have managed to hoard
the greatest amount of shiny metals
alone have the right
to rule?

The first, and greatest enemy of man
is the illusion of *self* which
he holds so dear.

Second, are the inter-national
cartel of banksters and
their friends.

Third, are
lawyers.

What's amazing
is how reliably selfishness
will lead a man to cowardice.

forget righteousness ———
in your time, war is not just a racket,
wars are the largest form of premeditated
organized crime… and in any fight,
especially the fixed ones,
there is a third party
who benefits.
who is it?
who is it we do not hear of?
who is it that *cannot* be criticized?
who is it in the shadows?
that's the enemy!
look, there!

88

The anxiety to be *perfect*
is what withers vegetation;
and the greater good is the chief law.
"Modernity" seems "forward-looking"
because modernity is reactionary;
reacting against the past.
But *who's* past?
Indeed:
in the beginning,
all the world was America!

I protected my naiveté
and saved a seat at the table
between Rousseau and Whitman,
where we convinced ourselves
that man is basically noble…
and only twisted by
institutions.
Then, once
the moment
of payments and
liberation from the past
arrived, how did we finally pay
for everything we had and
everything we were?
With *ceremony*.

In an attempt to unify Europe,
where the likes of Hitler and Napoleon
had failed with the use of sheer force —
the globalists succeed by *stealth*.

It would seem that the higher a man's status
the more he wishes to be humiliated,
and that God refuses to have
his work made manifest
by *cowards*.

The past always promises greater simplicity
to a man who feels that he is living with
the water at his neck; to every man
who realizes he is a fugitive
from nature.
History
is juvenile: in time,
it will coil up and bite its own tail.

"no more conflict! no more unequalness!
no more distinction between religions,
nor peoples, nor states, nor races!
no more man! no more woman!
no more criminals, nor heroes!
no more adventure, nor hate!
no more vengeance!
let there be only
eternal comfort
throughout
the ages!"

we carried our home
on our backs,
like snails;

the women were weaker,
but no less resilient
or resistant than
the best man;

and no one was valued as much
as the brother-in-arms able
to liberate us from
the greatest
torture of
war:

cold, sticky
tasteless
meals.

money is not a natural law,
and when any man-made system fails,
it becomes a *moral imperative* to scrap it —
a mathematical endless loop producing
huge levels of ever-expanding debt;
the way the game is designed,
there will always be debt, yet
never enough money to
pay it all off;
money *is*
debt.

૫૨

can men not see how we
have become entangled in our own nets?
Lord, free me! but o' —— *not yet!*

I met a childhood friend after half a lifetime,
and while I tried to talk to him about coffee
and the weather, he kept trying to convince
me that the world we live in is ruled in fact
by *words* with "hidden meanings", and that
the true state of human affairs reads much
like some horror movie script where trusted
and respected leaders of society secretly, and
often through blackmail, belong to what he
naively described as a satanic *cabal* gradually
turning all of humanity into mind-controlled
cattle, all-while making it appear totally
natural. Insisting that mankind now has a
terminal disease and that the People are in a
state of denial, once he began unpacking for
me the "evils of central banking" and the
"ugly truth behind the curtain at the end
of the Yellow Brick Road", I, at last, had
no choice but to interrupt my childhood
friend, politely as I could, and tell
him that he better learn how to
keep his God-damned
mouth shut.

accessible as it is,
the supermarket and grocery store
erodes something authentic toward which
our instincts point: the inherent need
to actively engage in gathering,
capturing, growing, and
killing our food.

Mistakes be made in order to learn from,
unless I be mistaken ———
'tis the main theme of the human story:
victims of our own creations.

To whom *exactly* are
all of these debts owed?
And where did our credit'rs
get all this money they loaned?

The urge of greed never inspired braveness;
know iron to be the same as gold.
Valuing life as vile as metal;
man is held by all he holds.

Become a fox
to discern the traps,
a lion to frighten hyenas;
the end *is* the means you use to
achieve it; keep the balance like a ballerina.

५६

The sheep turn their cheek so often,
their heads are on a swivel,
and the prime leaders
of their nations
are nothing more than
the most popular girls at
a high-end brothel for *elites*.

Common women truly
are full of much understanding;
they will quietly admit to themselves
that a virile young monk can't possibly
manage to *sweat* his seed out
through his *brain*.

५८

The importance of being fit enough to run,
without break, to your closet ally
cannot be *over*estimated;
preparing for the worst
is *always* worthwhile;
stay in sync with
your instincts.

૫૮

Nothing but praise
was addressed to that virtuous citizen
at which hour, *suddenly*, the situation
of Robespierre was reversed;
there's always gratitude
for the turner of tables
and the holy satire
of the French.

εο

The menace of his class
crashed the school's talent show,
spitting his truth before being taken down:

"I was forced to learn
how to feel like a woman;
they told me to be tame,
but I said I wouldn't.

I fell from being a king's son
to being a cook,
then they tried to hang me dead
for stealing a book.

I was forced to learn
how to feel like a woman;
they told me to be tame,
but I said I wouldn't.

Where a man's wound is,
his genius'll be;
there's no way out till'
you've paid the last penny.

I was forced to learn…"

This high and those curves are nothing;
the sciences of westerners are nothing;
the philosophies of easterners, and their
idol houses, are nothing. Transcend
the unseen, for this doubt and
surmise are: *nothing.* To be
in the world, and yet
escape from it;
to live only
after dying…
now *that*
is something.
Do you seek repose
for your soul? The soul's repose
is nothing. The tears shed for a companion?
That is something. The beauty of flesh lives
for a moment, in a moment no more;
the beauty of action and noble
ideals? That is something.
The oceanic feeling Freud
failed to tune into?
Now, *that...*

६२

our generation is the caravan
in which we move like
content captives.

६३

Quietly,
all nations
study and perfect
newer and ghastlier
means of annihilating
all their foes, wholesale;
the People must outlaw
any and all *secrecy*
concerning war
negotiations.

६४

I tested destiny's depth with both feet,
then taught the lion to tell his own tale;
I relied on my own taste
and faced the consequences,
then at last learned we can only hate
what we don't understand.

in the name of science,
which was never
supposed to be meant
for the objective of
bodily comforts,
whether we build gods
or our own exterminators...
our trajectory suggests
that man's destiny
is to be a *pet*.

ƐƐ

How easily suit and ties often forget
that *writing* marched alongside *weapons*.
they delude themselves into thinking that
there is some profound, substantial
distinction which raises them
above the primitive;
above the past.

they don't see how thin a veneer
"civilization" really is, and that
cannibal behavior's only ever
around the corner.

three days without bread,
nine missed meals,
chaos.

but if you ask the freemasons,
they'll tell you:
out of chaos,
is *order.*

the only secret is that there is no secret.

wah, hey guru!

Mary gave birth to Jesus during the spring.
Nimrod, however, *was* born on the 25th
of a December; <u>that</u> Nimrod who
had a Tower built in his kingdom
of Babel which would reach
so high it could allow man
to *taunt God!* ——
"they"
have you worshipping
something very different
from what you might believe.
Nimrod, too, was most passionate
about the idea of a One World Government.

And the damned tree…

It seems there really was
only ever *one* Christian,
and he died on the cross.

Those of Biblical faith must ask —
if there be a Devil, in contrast to a God,
how would we know we've been
possessed by him?

Merry Saturnalia, ya' filthy satanist.

६ट

it is the guarantee of many ancient sages:
if one can manage to stay awake with
the spine erect, all night long, one
will naturally be pushed toward
a spiritual frontier.

६८

I began to fear that vanity
is what really makes revolutions,
and that "liberty" is only ever a pretext —
just then, the tyrant planted his feet and
spoke to the bickering crowd, at last:

"Order…
is only the possibility of rest!
Come, do *you not desire rest now?*"

One of my favorite coincidences
is that we refer to, both electricity and
the force with which a people are kept
under the sway of a worldly leader,
by the exact same name: *POWER*.

killing the passions is no good,
nor will submission to them work;
they must be transformed alchemically
from base desires to noble ones;
physical lead must become
spiritual gold.

we call it a society, yet
go around professing, openly:
the totalest separation and isolation.
deeper, far deeper than
supply-and-demand,
are obligations
as sacred as
man's life
itself.

by what standard
will posterity
judge us?

ōm...

one says
compromise
is a synonym
for life itself;

another says
we will escape compromise
only in the paradise risen
from the ashes of
civilization;

I dare to point out
that sometimes… sometimes
it can even pay to be uncompromising.

98

Men are inclined to believe
that they cannot hold securely
whatever they possess... unless,
they get more at another's expense.

The very first lesson of politics
is that the political, in fact,
has *nothing* in common
with the moral —
first thing's
first:

> *"Right" lies in might.*

Law is the same
brutal, blind force which
shaped humanity's beginnings;
only in a collared, euphemistic disguise.

> *"Right" lies in might.*

Your rights, her rights,
he's right, our rights!
The *word* "right" is an abstraction
proved by nothing! —
but to be fair,
only the one trained from *childhood*
to rule over an entire mass of peoples,
can ever have a fluent grasp
of all the bullshit words
which may be made up
of political alphabets.

If you ask Nature,
she will tell you:
might is right.

On one hand: if a strong man
comes along and exploits the weak ——
Nature only shrugs: "might is right."

On the other hand:
if an even stronger man
comes along and destroys the exploiter,
serving justice to the weak and exploited ——
Nature, with goosebumps, raves:
"might is right."

Justice is heavy, and can only be served
by those who innerstand that
when we pray ask Nature,
all She ever says is:
"might is right."

Nature and Destiny both
favor the man with might.
"Right, right, right!"

99

The present only harvests
what the past has sown,
and the things we fear
have fears of their own.

"I swear to you, gentlemen:
to be overly conscious
is a *disease*…
and as such,
alcohol is God's apology
for making man self-aware!"

The drunk Scotsman then swore
to be a wild rover no more,
and launched his half-eaten pupusa
at the group of Israelis seated across him.

You may prefer
to ride a horse,
but there are
cabbages to
be planted.

to

daily, I sang hymns of praise
and made austere preparations
to welcome glorious death, like
a bride awaiting her groom's
return from the frontier.

If you're going to be wrong,
be wrong at 150 miles an hour;
if you're going to hit a wall,
leave a massive hole in it;
and if you're standing on thin ice…
might as well *dance*.

'Tis true:
no matter how we act
or who we pretend to be,
we all wish to feel understood,
preferably by a beautiful woman ——
but these are things which
life does not owe a man;
one can only be
prepared to
appreciate its
magnificence
when it happens.

Have a little pity on the pessimist.

တ၃

Among the million eggs a fly might lay,
very few will hatch… and yet
the race of the flies
thrives.

No — fire cannot be fought with fire,
but know that force will indeed be
extinguished only with force;
and violence with violence;
and property with
expropriation.

"I solemnly swear I have *tried*
turning the other cheek,
but henceforth will exact
an eye for a tooth and
a head for an eye…
if it be Your will,
amen."

impotent minds,
though they might *hear*,
do not absorb the teachings
into their memory — and, instead,
show us the way water seeps
from a leaking jar.
defilements
of mine mind, like
dacoits before the monsoon,
robbed me blind, and seeking salvation,
I pursued a self-proclaimed holy man
who, upon hearing mine ordeal,
proclaimed that all tyranny is
voluntary — then, he lit
a match and served me
the chillum.

τε

Practically speaking:
do you know *exactly*
what caused the downfall
of the ancient "Western" world?

The fall of the birth-rate,
is at the bottom of
everything.

The ruling class had grown wealthy,
urbanized, and tame *past precedent*.
Consequentially, inspired by the
wish to ensure a life free from
care for their heirs, rulers
quickly learned that this
entails: the more heirs,
the less each receive.

Maybe idleness
and living off of others
leads to a potent desire to command.

tt

the People helped build themselves a prison
as the money lenders spectated
from the shadows;
soon enough,
the inmates were told
that if they didn't police themselves well,
they would not advance in life
and life would just not
get any better.

the People did not learn in time that
you cannot *comply* your way
out of tyranny.

just as the freedom which
our rulers promise is,
in truth, slavery ———
the understanding which
our rulers promise is,
in truth, confusion.

88

one thing
Dante never considered
is that hell would be a place
the overwhelming majority *love*.

to

The more a man judges,
the less he can love —
the more people talk about it,
the less consensus there can be.

The secret to *autonomy*
lies in enlightening men,
whilst the secret to tyranny
lies in keeping them ignorant.

And to be sure:
conspiracy is the most
ill-advised path toward revolution.

A mother received complaint
from many fellow townsfolk that
her son had been causing mischief;
she sat him down forthwith,
and advised him to:
"remember —
whatever shuts a man away
from the waterfall and the wildcat
will ultimately kill him… and
the most reliable route to
disillusionment is to
have had enough —
to get your fill."

Without sincere leaders who do as they say,
laws on paper become mere words on paper;
and words, at their best, lead to truthsome
falsehoods — never the *whole* truth.
Like a mathematician's dilemma
to wonder what else can
be relied on besides
formal systems, 'tis
a buddha's dilemma
to wonder what else
there is to rely on
besides *words*:
souvenirs of
the tongue.
Ōm…

੯੩

a genuine anarchist who wants freedom
for both himself and the world,
will discover that every man
has to free himself
by himself;
and,
as if that
were not enough,
the anarchist begins to see
that if a man is born into slavery,
freedom, being contrary to his nature,
becomes another sort of tyranny for him.
and if even a society, in which only
the natural qualities of men are
in effect, becomes a heap of
tyrannies — who
will we blame?

devils are at a discount in the bāzār
and celebrities are our gods now,
so, rightfully —— no one
will come to help us; but
the prize to be won is
all of humanity
reaching out
towards its
collective
mighty
spirit.

Imagine a politicking in which
politicians can't be bought.
Imagine a free media who
considers it its *dharma*
to tell the truth.
Imagine,
if you can:
banks accountable
to the People, and a free market
where everyone has access to the same
information at the same time.
Imagine all the people…
living-life-in-peace,
woohoo*!*

٩٥

I organized and equipped my soul
for action; swept away the old for the new;
embracing that there'd be no satisfaction,
relying on band-aids for bullet wounds.

Never asked the sun for any mercy,
never mapped all the province I explored;
strength is sanctioned to those
who are worthy, and o'
the labor... is its
own reward.

There are no strangers,
there are no friends:
repeat this and
forget your
name —
forget
the means,
just reach the end;
deep sleep is for the tame.

There are no strangers,
there are no friends...

ॐ

Give me four brave idealists
who recognize the sentiment of
making revolution *for its own sake* —
and then get the hell out of the way, man!

tt

What's the difference between
retirement homes, public schooling,
zoos, and prisons? I don't know either.
In the end: the elderly were still taken to
the mountain to be left for dead, children
only received initiation into a mutilated life,
and elephants proved far too gun-shy for
use in exploiting others… but in prison,
somehow, hope survived. Indeed,
the elders became quality fertilizer,
the children were pimped out
to the elite, and the elephants
were slaughtered for nothing
more than jewelry… but
out of the prison came
monks, musicians,
and barbarians.
"Reform"

ᛐᛐ

(a chorus of soldiers marching,
but in the style of a lullaby)

they say "don't you steal",
we say: don't let em' steal from you.
responsibility's what they fear,
and courage: what they lack.
the dogs continue barking,
the caravan continues to pass.

the time to be naive
ended with Eve;
there is no time for sleep…
we've got her apple.

they say "don't you steal",
we say: don't let em steal from you.
responsibility's what they fear,
courage: what they lack.
the dogs continue barking,
the caravan continues to pass.

900

The living forces of evil
are to be found in the ideals of our day;
but, rest assured that after the death
of his last victim, the vampire,
sooner or later, dies too.

Discover the jellyfish within,
and do your own heart's bidding.
With stubbornness, take *those* paths
which timid souls will be sure to evade.
Between a laugh and a cry, observe
in awe: a herd of men digging
their own graves…
and the rest,
stealing bones
to crawl away with
and gnaw at, unobserved. "Urine
can be analyzed, but not the soul!"
Not for fear of hardship nor love of ease,
as necessary as it may seem, is compromise
ever worth it. Never swallow pills of shame,
nor ever serve a dose to anyone else.
How, then, to treat others?
There are no others.